How many tiny hidden Baxter the Bumblebees like this  *can you find throughout the book?*

Check out page 98 for the answer!

This part is for the big kids......parents and teachers!

You've picked up this activity book because, like us you believe children are 'Born 2 Succeed'. Within every child, there are seeds of greatness and amazing potential. But like all seeds, this potential must be planted, nurtured and protected. Part of tending to these seeds of greatness and seeing them come to fruition means learning some life lessons. Life lessons are those lessons we must all learn at some stage; we can either learn to just get by, or we can triumph. We want your child to triumph and become all they were meant to be!

This activity book is designed to accompany the storybook 'Baxter Learns to Fly.' It's another tool you can use to help open communication channels with children when navigating the life lessons shared in the storybook —like learning not to let the negative words of others define their future. Other lessons include showing empathy, kindness, building resilience, celebrating our differences, and being patient.

You can use the wisdom tips opposite each colouring picture along with Baxter's own experience with negative words to help your child navigate difficult experiences, emotions or thoughts. Colouring together provides a connection point and can lower the intensity of emotionally challenging conversations and may even make learning some difficult life lessons more fun. Baxter and his friends can also be a practical example for you to use and children to relate to when they navigate difficult times and experiences.

Life Lessons...

Where 'Baxter Learns to Fly' differs from other children's storybooks is the focus on life lessons. The main life lesson in 'Baxter Learns to Fly' is...don't let other people's negative words become your self-talk and limit or define your future. We believe that what children hear, they will speak, what they speak, they will believe, and what they believe they will become. It is so important that our children hear positive, encouraging words from us and they develop positive, kind talk about themselves and others because this is what they will believe and ultimately what they will become.

There are many great ways to teach your children difficult lessons to prepare them for the future, but when you have a tool to facilitate that learning, and one that children can relate to, it can make things a whole lot easier!

The story goes like this...

In the story 'Baxter Learns to Fly', Baxter the Bumblebee experienced the pain of unkind and negative words spoken to him from someone he admired. Maxwell the Mosquito laughed at Baxter and told him his wings were too small to fly.

Baxter and his friends Lydia the Ladybug and Boston the Butterfly had always dreamed of going to 'Bug Flying School' to learn to fly together, but when Baxter heard these negative words, he believed Maxwell and decided to go home instead. Baxter almost missed out on going to 'Bug Flying School' by letting Maxwell's negative words define his future.

But, Baxter's mother taught him that although Maxwell was correct in saying bumblebees do have small wings compared to their big fluffy bodies, it was not the whole truth when he said bumblebees can't fly because of their tiny wings. The truth is bumblebees can fly and they can carry large amounts of pollen to make honey too!

The Moral of the Story...

The moral of this story is: words are powerful so be careful how you use them. Choose them wisely and choose them to encourage and build yourself and others up.

Building your children up...

Words can encourage and build up, or they can tear down and wound, especially 'little' hearts that have not yet learned ways of coping with these hurts. For parents and teachers, it can be difficult helping children navigate different life lessons, heartaches, adversity, and the whole range of complex emotions and events that they will encounter as they grow older.

We encourage you to read through the links to the story as well as the wisdom tips first, then set some time aside to plan for the connection points before sharing them with your children. This will help you be fully prepared to talk through the life lessons while you enjoy colouring in together – making things more fun. You are welcome to photocopy the pictures and use them to colour in together or with a group of your children's friends or even a whole class as you discuss the corresponding life lesson.

Being a Good Friend.

In our story 'Baxter Learns to Fly'...

Baxter had two good friends: Lydia the Ladybug and Boston the Butterfly. The three bugs looked quite different from each other. Lydia had long sleek wings that hid under her hard shell when she wasn't using them. Boston had big, wide, colourful wings, and Baxter had small, delicate wings. The three bugs were excited because finally they were going to 'Bug Flying School' to learn to fly together.

Wisdom tip for parents and teachers:

Making friends, having friends, and being a friend are all important parts of a child's development. Apart from the obvious need for connection and company, there are many other social, emotional and physical benefits to building friendships. It is important for children to learn the skills to develop and nurture friendships like doing things together, learning to share, considering how others feel (empathy), being kind and helpful even when others are not kind to us, and listening to each other.

Connection Point:

- Ask your children: Who are some of your friends?
- What are some of the things you like best about your friends?
- What sort of things do you like to do with your friends?
- What does being a good friend mean? Are you a good friend?

Friendship

Can you find these words in the puzzle?

baxter	happy	laugh
boston	help	share
empathy	kind	
friend	listen	

Can you complete these sentences using the words from the puzzle?

* I am a good f_____, because I am k___ with my words and actions.

* Being a good friend makes me h____.

a	h	b	n	b	o	s	t	o	n	h
z	e	m	p	a	t	h	y	c	h	a
l	l	n	m	x	v	c	q	w	e	p
i	p	b	m	t	k	i	n	d	m	p
s	h	a	r	e	m	p	a	t	h	y
t	p	o	f	r	i	e	n	d	c	w
e	l	a	u	g	h	s	s	x	n	m
n	a	e	i	s	h	a	r	e	o	u

A friend is one of the nicest things to have and one of the nicest things to be.

Understanding what is correct and what is the TRUTH!

In our story 'Baxter Learns to Fly'...

Baxter met with Maxwell the Mosquito on his way to 'Bug Flying School'. Baxter proudly announced to Maxwell that he was going to learn to fly. Maxwell laughed at him and told him that was impossible because bumblebees had wings that were too small to keep their big fluffy bodies up in the air. What Maxwell said was correct...bumblebees do have small wings, but it wasn't THE truth. Bumblebees CAN fly!

Wisdom tip for parents and teachers:

Our children will go through life hearing things that are technically correct but not necessarily the truth. In their formative years, we can help our children interpret what is correct and what is THE TRUTH. For example, "you can't walk, so you can't play." It may be correct that you can't walk, but you most certainly CAN play...you just need to change how you play. "You look different because you came from a different country, so you don't belong." It may be correct that you came from a different country and you look different to some others, but the truth is, you don't have to be the same to belong. The truth is, you look different to me and we all belong.

Connection Point:

- As you colour in the picture together, talk to your children about things that are technically true and what is THE TRUTH.

- Take this opportunity to talk about things your children have heard about themselves or others that are technically true but are not THE TRUTH!

Correct versus the truth

Can you find these words in the puzzle?

baxter	help	truth
boston	honest	right
correct	kind	
good	true	

Can you complete these sentences using the words from the puzzle?

* It is g____ to always tell the t___h.

* Maxwell was c__r__t when he said Baxter had small wings ..... but that did not mean he couldn't fly.

* The t____ is, Baxter could fly!

q	w	c	k	i	n	d	r	g
s	b	o	s	t	o	n	s	o
v	a	r	h	e	l	p	b	o
n	x	r	o	t	r	u	e	d
m	t	e	n	r	i	g	h	t
c	e	c	e	u	l	o	i	u
o	r	t	s	t	z	x	q	u
e	a	i	t	h	o	u	c	d

Hint: Look for words that go down the page (vertical) and words that go across the page (horizontal)

Create your best future!

In our story 'Baxter Learns to Fly'...

Baxter met Maxwell the Mosquito on his way to 'Bug Flying School'. Baxter told Maxwell that he was going to learn to fly, just like him! Baxter admired Maxwell because he was an expert flyer, so when Maxwell laughed at Baxter and told him he couldn't fly, it made Baxter sad and it hurt his feelings. Since Maxwell had already been to 'Bug Flying School' and was an expert flyer, Baxter believed him and almost gave up on learning to fly!

Wisdom tip for parents and teachers:

When someone laughs at or makes fun of us, it hurts our feelings, especially if that person is someone we admire or look up to. But, we have a choice. We can either believe them and let those negative words shape our future, OR we can choose not to believe them and create our own positive future! Words are powerful and they can build up or tear down. So, if our children hear negative words spoken about them, we must replace those negative words with the truth and with positive words. We can acknowledge the truth and frame it positively.

Connection Point:

- When your children hear negative words spoken about them, teach them a motto to kindly reply with. They can say it out loud and repeat it silently to themselves. Practice the motto you create with them, so they are prepared next time someone says something negative.

   For example: "I do have small delicate wings, and I can fly AND carry lots of pollen too!" .... OR ....."I can't run like you but I can paint amazing colourful pictures and tell funny stories." Always focus on the positive.

Create your best future!

Can you find these words in the puzzle?

baxter   future   lydia
boston   good   positive
build   great
create   hope

Can you complete these sentences using the words from the puzzle?

* I c___te my future with my words.

* I will say only p_____ve words about my future. My f_____ is going to be gr___!

b	a	x	t	e	r	h	b	c
o	l	y	d	i	a	o	u	r
s	c	v	b	n	x	p	i	e
t	f	u	t	u	r	e	l	a
o	d	f	g	h	j	k	d	t
n	p	o	s	i	t	i	v	e
c	v	g	r	e	a	t	t	y
z	a	q	u	g	o	o	d	b

Use kind and positive words when you speak about yourself and others.
You create your future with your words!

Be careful who you spend your time with.

In our story 'Baxter Learns to Fly'...

When Maxwell the Mosquito told Baxter he couldn't fly, Baxter felt sad. Ever since he was a baby bumblebee, Baxter dreamed of flying, so the thought that he was never going to fly was heartbreaking for him.

Baxter spent too long listening to Maxwell convincing him that he would never be able to fly... so much so that he decided to go home instead of going to 'Bug Flying School' with Lydia and Boston. Fortunately, Mother Bumblebee showed Baxter he could fly!

Wisdom tip for parents and teachers:

We need to teach our children to be careful who they spend their time with. If we spend our time with negative people who only sow negativity into our lives, we will begin to think negatively too.

Mahatma Gandhi said, "Keep your thoughts positive...your thoughts become your words. Keep your words positive...your words become your behaviour. Keep your behaviour positive...your behaviour becomes your habits. Keep your habits positive...your habits become your values. Keep your values positive...your values become your destiny."

Connection Point:

- Using Baxter as an example, talk to your children about the people they spend time with. Are these people sowing positive words and deeds into their lives?

- Spend some time teaching your children to gracefully remove themselves from negative situations if possible, or to kindly steer a conversation in a more positive direction.

Be careful who you spend your time with.

Can you find these words in the puzzle?

alert	boston	time
aware	careful	spend
baxter	guarded	
become	lydia	

Can you complete these sentences using the words from the puzzle?

* You be____ like the people you sp___ your time with. Spend time with positive people!

* Baxter had 2 positive friends called B____n and Ly___.

q	w	c	a	r	e	f	u	l	v
v	b	n	l	r	t	y	g	y	z
c	a	r	e	f	u	l	u	d	t
c	w	f	r	r	t	y	a	i	i
b	a	x	t	e	r	x	r	a	m
a	r	s	p	e	n	d	d	v	e
b	e	c	o	m	e	b	e	v	b
r	b	o	s	t	o	n	d	m	p

You become like the people you spend most of your time with, so choose those people carefully!

It's okay to feel sad but no self-pity here!

In our story 'Baxter Learns to Fly'...

When Baxter was told by Maxwell the Mosquito that he couldn't fly because his wings were too small, he felt sad and he cried. Baxter believed what Maxwell told him, so he decided he was going to go home and not go to 'Bug Flying School'...or even try to fly.

Wisdom tip for parents and teachers:

When someone says something negative or unkind to us, it hurts our feelings. It is natural to feel sad, and it is okay to show emotion and cry, but it's not okay to stay in a place of self-pity. Self-pity is a destructive emotion that can stop us from achieving our dreams. It forces us to look back and experience the hurt again. What we need to do is to look forward to the many amazing possibilities that lie ahead of us. Baxter believed something that wasn't the whole truth, but Mother Bumblebee got him back on track, believing he could fly.

Connection Point:

- When something sad happens, let your children explain what has upset them, correct any misunderstanding (like Baxter's mum did), and then turn their thoughts to the positive things that they <u>can</u> do.

- Make a 'can do' list with your children. Start by writing down all the things that they can do. When their feelings and thoughts turn to the negative, help them refocus on the positive. It takes time, but this is a good discipline to learn.

Sad versus self-pity.

Can you find these words in the puzzle?

baxter	hope	selfpity
boston	lydia	succeed
choice	option	
happy	sad	

Can you complete these sentences using the words from the puzzle?

* It is okay to feel s__ for a while but we can make a ch___e to be h___y.

* Baxter felt sad for a while and almost gave up on his dream. But he didn't stay in s___-p___. Ba____ went back to Bug Flying School to learn to fly!

a	s	e	l	f	p	i	t	y
b	a	s	c	g	b	e	z	l
g	d	j	h	h	a	p	p	y
b	r	m	o	o	x	s	s	d
o	l	k	i	p	t	d	s	i
s	u	c	c	e	e	d	n	a
t	z	x	e	b	r	z	x	c
o	p	t	i	o	n	l	h	g
n	x	f	d	s	a	q	w	e

Self-pity will stop you from being all you should and could be.

Good things about being different!

In our story 'Baxter Learns to Fly'...

Baxter looked different to his friends Lydia and Boston. Lydia was shiny and black with long sleek wings. Boston had big, wide and beautiful wings. Baxter had always been proud of his small, delicate wings and his big, round, fluffy body...that was until Maxwell the Mosquito laughed at his tiny wings and told him that they were too small to keep his big fluffy body up in the air! Baxter began comparing himself to his friends and wondered if he was good enough. This almost made him miss out on going to 'Bug Flying School'.

Wisdom tip for parents and teachers:

It's human nature to compare. Comparing in itself isn't unhealthy, it's natural. However, we can learn to compare in a positive way, looking for the good things about being different and framing our thoughts positively.

For example, Baxter could say, "I don't have long sleek wings that hide under a pretty shell like Lydia," or he could say, "I do have wings that are different to yours, they are delicate but they are strong enough to keep my fabulously fluffy body up in the air and I can carry large amounts of pollen too!"

Connection Point:

- Make a list with your children of things they like about themselves.
- Make a list with your children about some of the things they are good at or can do well.
- Teach your children a personal motto focusing on the things they are good at.

Look for the good things about being different!

Can you find these words in the puzzle?

baxter	good	unique
boston	grateful	unlike
different	lydia	
diversity	positive	

Can you complete these sentences using the words from the puzzle?

* Being di_____nt means I am u____e and therefore special!

* Diver____ is g___ and exciting!

26

q	w	e	r	g	o	o	d	b	g
p	n	u	s	l	y	d	i	a	r
o	u	n	l	i	k	e	v	m	a
s	d	i	f	f	e	r	e	n	t
i	v	q	h	s	d	q	r	b	e
t	c	u	a	s	d	m	s	o	f
i	v	e	b	n	m	h	i	s	u
v	b	a	x	t	e	r	t	t	l
e	u	n	i	q	u	e	y	o	x
n	d	i	f	f	e	r	e	n	t

"Start each day with a positive thought and a grateful heart."
Roy T Bennett

Showing Empathy.

In our story 'Baxter Learns to Fly'...

Baxter was sad after Maxwell told him he would never fly because his wings were too small. But Baxter's loyal friends Boston and Lydia were there to support him.

Wisdom tip for parents and teachers:

Learning empathy and how to be a loyal friend is important.

Baxter's friends, Lydia and Boston, were empathic by encouraging, comforting and supporting Baxter.

Empathy *[noun]* ...the ability to understand and share the feelings of another.

Boston and Lydia wanted to learn to fly just as much as Baxter, so they understood Baxter's sadness when Maxwell told him that bumblebees couldn't fly.

Lydia and Boston could have just continued to 'Bug Flying School' to achieve their own dream of flying, but they didn't. They stopped to care for Baxter.

Connection Point:

- Using Lydia and Boston as examples, take this opportunity to talk to your children about what empathy is. Have they ever seen someone sad? How did it make them feel? What did they do?

- Make a plan with your children to show empathy to others in a safe way. What can they do? Who can they ask for help? What encouraging words of kindness can they say?

Showing Empathy

Can you find these words in the puzzle?

baxter	friend	love
boston	good	sensitive
compassion	help	
empathy	kind	

Can you complete these sentences using the words from the puzzle?

* Always be k___ and sensitive to the needs of others.

* Boston and Lydia showed em____y and compassion when Ba____ felt sad.

z	b	e	x	b	b	n	m	g	l
c	o	m	p	a	s	s	i	o	n
r	s	p	g	x	i	s	s	o	m
q	t	a	w	t	e	r	t	d	t
v	o	t	b	e	k	h	c	d	e
f	n	h	f	r	i	e	n	d	z
q	u	y	b	v	n	l	o	v	e
z	x	q	u	m	d	p	c	d	e
s	e	n	s	i	t	i	v	e	a

Empathy means to consider how others might feel and be kind.

Comparing kills confidence!

In our story 'Baxter Learns to Fly'...

Baxter was told by Maxwell the Mosquito that he would never fly because his wings were too small. Baxter had always been proud of his small delicate wings but now he wished he was more like his friends Lydia the Ladybug and Boston the Butterfly who had bigger wings.

Wisdom tip for parents and teachers:

When we compare ourselves to others too much, it kills our confidence and steals our joy. We stop looking at the beauty and uniqueness in ourselves and we stop being grateful for all that we do have. When we make a deliberate effort to be grateful for the amazing, unique and beautiful qualities we possess, the skills and abilities we do have, and the possessions however great or small we have, we develop an attitude of gratitude and this brings inner joy. There is nothing wrong with aiming higher, striving for more, and admiring certain qualities in others, but don't let this become a self-critical exercise and steal your joy. The only person you should compare yourself to...is you!

Connection Point:

- Using Baxter as an example, spend some time talking about comparing ourselves to others. In what ways do you compare yourself to others? Does this take your joy away?

- Make a list with your child about the things they like about themselves and a list of things they admire in three friends.

- Make a list with your child of five things they are grateful for. You might like to do this yourself too!

33

Comparing kills confidence!

Can you find these words in the puzzle?

amazing	confidence	special
awesome	compare	unique
baxter	future	
boston	lydia	

Can you complete these sentences using the words from the puzzle?

* I am am_____ and u_____. I don't need to compare myself to anyone else!

* Baxter didn't need to c_____e his wings to Boston's or Lydia's. His wings were very sp_____!

a	c	a	w	e	s	o	m	e
c	o	m	p	a	r	e	s	o
s	n	a	b	o	s	t	o	n
p	f	z	a	l	x	z	u	p
e	i	i	x	y	v	b	n	q
c	d	n	t	d	n	m	i	s
i	e	g	e	i	d	q	q	u
a	n	v	r	a	s	n	u	p
l	c	f	u	t	u	r	e	o
r	e	z	x	f	r	e	s	t

'You won't be distracted by comparison if you are captivated by your purpose.'
Author unknown

Always show kindness even when you feel sad.

In our story 'Baxter Learns to Fly'...

After listening to Maxwell the Mosquito telling him he couldn't fly because his wings were too small, Baxter decided to go home and not go to 'Bug Flying School'. On the way home, Baxter met Susie the Spider again. Baxter was sad when he stood talking to Susie, but he still found something nice to say to Susie. Baxter told Susie that he liked her pretty web.

Wisdom tip for parents and teachers:

When we feel sad, it is easy to look at the negative side of most things, and it can be even easier to see more negative things in ourselves or believe the negative, hurtful words others have said to us.

But, even when we are hurting, if we can do or say something nice or kind to someone else, it makes us feel good too. Our amazing bodies release a hormone called oxytocin, which has many health benefits as well as making us feel good.

Connection Point:

- Plan two random acts of kindness for you and your child to do for someone else.

- Plan some random kind things to say to others. For example, "I like your hair," or "I like your jumper." There is always something nice you can find to say about or to everyone.

- Make a plan with your child to respond with something kind and positive in response to negative or hurtful words spoken to them.

Always show kindness

Can you find these words in the puzzle?

always	gentle	powerful
baxter	good	sensitive
boston	help	
change	kindness	

Can you complete these sentences using the words from the puzzle?

* Always be sen_____ to how others feel and show kindness when you h___ them.

* Even when Baxter felt sad, he still showed ki_____ to Susie the Spider, telling her that her web was pretty.

g	o	o	d	a	d	g	h	j	s
e	p	o	w	e	r	f	u	l	e
n	h	e	l	p	q	w	e	r	n
t	f	j	z	x	m	c	r	k	s
l	p	c	h	a	n	g	e	i	i
e	b	a	x	t	e	r	z	n	t
a	l	w	a	y	s	q	m	d	i
v	b	y	b	o	s	t	o	n	v
k	i	n	d	n	e	s	s	z	e

"Unexpected kindness is the most powerful, least costly and most underrated agent of human change."
Bob Kerrey

Share your burdens

In our story 'Baxter Learns to Fly'...

Baxter came home incredibly sad after Maxwell the Mosquito told him he would never be able to fly because his wings were too small. After arriving home, Baxter told his mum why he felt sad and what Maxwell had said. Mother Bumblebee was wise, and she understood the struggles and effort it took to learn to fly. She listened patiently to Baxter with empathy and kindness...but then she encouraged Baxter and showed him bumblebees can fly, so of course he could learn to fly too!

Wisdom tip for parents and teachers:

When we share our burdens with someone we trust or someone that we know cares for us, it reduces the sadness we feel, especially when that person shows empathy and kindness and encourages us. Encouragement helps us see better options, new possibilities and the truth! What other people say about you does not define who you are. You are amazing, gifted, talented and unique. So next time, when someone you care for experiences the pain of negative words and shares their burden with you, choose to show empathy and encourage them to see new possibilities and a brighter future.

Connection Point:

- Using Baxter as an example, talk to your children about ways they share their burdens and with whom.

- Now, talk to your children about how they show empathy to others when others are sharing their burdens or sadness with them. What do they do? How do they show kindness and empathy and how do they encourage others?

Share your burdens

Can you find these words in the puzzle?

baxter	care	help
boston	encourage	trust
brighter	feel	
burdens	future	

Can you complete these sentences using the words from the puzzle?

* When others are feeling sad, h___ them to share their burdens.

* Ba____ shared his bu_____ with his mum.

b	r	i	g	h	t	e	r	z	x
u	p	o	h	b	g	f	b	d	h
r	e	n	c	o	u	r	a	g	e
d	t	r	u	s	t	d	x	k	l
e	a	s	d	t	n	b	t	v	p
n	s	s	d	o	b	f	e	e	l
s	v	c	v	n	c	a	r	e	x
f	u	t	u	r	e	b	v	d	s

'A burden shared is a burden halved.'

Be proud to be you!

In our story 'Baxter Learns to Fly'...

Maxwell the Mosquito told Baxter that his wings were too small to keep his big fluffy body up in the air, so he would never be able to fly. Baxter had always been proud of his small wings, until now.

Baxter admired Lydia the Ladybug's long sleek wings. She could easily fold them up and hide them under her black spotted shell when she wasn't using them. Baxter wished his wings were bigger like Lydia's.

Wisdom tip for parents and teachers:

A bumblebee's job is to collect pollen from flowers to make honey, so they need strong wings to help them carry these heavy loads. They fly by moving their wings in a circular pattern, like a helicopter, and they beat their wings up to 200 times per second. If Baxter had big wings like Lydia or Boston, he wouldn't be able to beat his wings fast enough to fly and carry the pollen he needs to make honey!

We are all different, unique and special. We have different gifts and talents. We look different, we think differently, we come from different countries, we like different foods, and we have different goals, dreams and aspirations. Being different is good! It's exciting and fun. Admire the differences in others but be proud to be you!

Connection Point:

- Ask your children to write down one thing they admire about everyone in their family or class at school.

- Now, make a list with your children of the things that make them different from others. Have a celebration party together, sharing those differences with each other. Remember, we are all unique and special, and THAT is worth celebrating!

Be proud to be you!

Can you find these words in the puzzle?

admire	different	special
baxter	flowers	unique
boston	honey	
care	lydia	

Can you complete these sentences using the words from the puzzle?

* We are all dif_____ and uni___. That makes us all spe____.

* Baxter's wings were small but they were strong. They helped him collect and carry lots of pollen from f___ers to make ho___.

b	o	s	t	o	n	b	n	b	b
l	a	d	m	i	r	e	z	h	a
y	u	n	i	q	u	e	c	o	x
d	d	i	f	f	e	r	e	n	t
i	c	a	r	e	z	p	t	e	e
a	q	w	e	r	t	y	u	y	r
f	l	o	w	e	r	s	b	v	c
f	g	s	p	e	c	i	a	l	g

Admire the differences in others but always be proud to be you!

Be sensitive to other people's abilities.

In our story 'Baxter Learns to Fly'...

Boston was a kind friend to Baxter. When Baxter listened to the negative words of Maxwell the Mosquito, Boston comforted Baxter and encouraged him to try to learn to fly. He even said to Baxter that "maybe Maxwell was wrong and bumblebees really can fly". Boston had beautiful wide wings that could easily keep his slender body up in the air so it was a sure thing that he would become an expert flyer! Boston could have gone off to 'Bug Flying School' by himself to realise his own dream of flying, but he didn't. He stopped and cared.

Wisdom tip for parents and teachers:

There are times in our lives when we will find that some things come easily to us. Our abilities may exceed those of others and the challenge of doing things may be lower for us.

It is during these times that we need to be sensitive to those around us and adjust our behaviour to support and care for them. Boston still went to 'Bug Flying School' so he didn't let others limit his destiny, but he was sensitive to Baxter's feelings and abilities and took time to be kind and encourage him.

Connection Point:

- Using Boston as an example, talk to your children about their abilities and what may come easier to them than to some others. How do they stop and care for those who are struggling in the areas that they find easy? This may be in an area of physical ability or in learning.

- Make a plan with your children to offer ways of reaching out to care for others who may be struggling in the areas that they find easier or excel in.

Be sensitive to other people's abilities.

Can you find these words in the puzzle?

ability	challenge	kind
baxter	disability	sensitive
boston	easy	
care	friend	

Can you complete these sentences using the words from the puzzle?

* Being a good fr____ means being sen____ve to others.

* When Ba____ thought he couldn't fly, Boston was a k___ friend and encouraged him.

d	i	s	a	b	i	l	i	t	y
z	x	e	q	w	e	e	b	t	y
j	h	n	g	f	d	a	a	s	e
b	o	s	t	o	n	s	x	f	b
a	b	i	l	i	t	y	t	r	n
t	r	t	e	w	p	o	e	i	z
v	c	i	t	r	c	a	r	e	p
q	w	v	r	t	n	b	v	n	c
m	n	e	b	v	k	i	n	d	c
c	h	a	l	l	e	n	g	e	n

~~Disability~~ - Different Ability.
We can all do something. Celebrate what you can do.

Be positive about your future!

In our story 'Baxter Learns to Fly'...

Baxter looked at his tiny delicate wings and compared them to the big wings of his friends, Boston the Butterfly and Lydia the Ladybug. But, Mother Bumblebee reminded Baxter that all bugs are different. Some bugs can fly and some can't, like Susie the Spider. Susie will never fly, but she can make beautiful sparkling webs. Casper the Caterpillar will fly one day, but he must be patient and wait until he comes out of his cocoon and grows his wings to fly. We all have different abilities, and this makes us unique and special. Baxter learned not to compare himself to others but to appreciate his own wings. This gave Baxter the confidence to go back to 'Bug Flying School' to learn to fly!

Wisdom tip for parents and teachers:

Our world is full of people with different abilities. Some can run, while others can't. Some can hula hoop, while others find it a struggle. Some can see and hear, while others can't. What other people say and think you can or cannot do does not define your future. Irrespective of your abilities, you define your future, so be positive about it.

Connection Point:

- Using Baxter and his friends, Susie the Spider and Casper the Caterpillar, as examples, talk with your children honestly about their different abilities.

- There may be some things that your children do well and other things they cannot do or will never be able to do. There may be other things that may take longer for them to do. Reassure them that it is okay, and that they are amazing! We are all different and there is always something we are good at. Get your children to write down what they are good at.

Be positive about your future!

Can you find these words in the puzzle?

afraid	different	strength
baxter	longer	wait
beautiful	persevere	
casper	positive	

Can you complete these sentences using the words from the puzzle?

* Sometimes learning new things is hard. Don't be af____. Pers_____, and keep trying.

* Sometimes we have to w____ for things. Ca_____ the Caterpillar had to wait until he turned into a butterfly before he could fly. Casper was happy and pos_____ about his future.

d	r	b	l	o	n	g	e	r	b
i	p	e	r	s	e	v	e	r	e
f	o	a	v	b	w	a	i	t	s
f	s	u	q	w	e	r	t	y	t
e	i	t	b	a	x	t	e	r	r
r	t	i	z	f	v	b	n	m	e
e	i	f	r	r	s	s	z	x	n
n	v	u	c	a	s	p	e	r	g
t	e	l	v	i	a	s	t	i	t
q	v	b	j	d	m	n	b	v	h

"A hero is an ordinary individual who finds the strength to persevere and endure in spite of overwhelming obstacles."
Christopher Reeve

Make time to celebrate!

In our story 'Baxter Learns to Fly'...

Baxter came home sad after Maxwell the Mosquito told him that he would never be able to fly because his wings were too small. When Baxter arrived home, his mother was in the kitchen baking a cake to celebrate. Baxter's mother knew that learning to fly was difficult and that there would be some troubles or crashes along the way. She was determined, however, to celebrate with Baxter and his friends because trying your best and not being afraid to try is something worth celebrating.

Wisdom tip for parents and teachers:

Making time to celebrate accomplishments, no matter how big or small, is important. Even our failures and mistakes can be celebrated as stepping stones to our next great success. Failures and mistakes can teach us new ways of thinking, empathy, innovation, creativity and kindness. Celebrating can make trying new things less scary and more fun!

Connection Point:

- When was the last time you celebrated an achievement with your child?

- How do you teach your child to approach mistakes and failures? Are they something to fear, or something to celebrate? We encourage you to celebrate, because now you have an opportunity to try again...a different way...a better way!

- Make a plan to celebrate your child's next achievement or their next mistake. Either way, they have learned something new. Set an example by celebrating your achievements and mistakes too.

Always make time to celebrate!

Can you find these words in the puzzle?

baxter	life	teach
best	mistakes	trying
celebrate	steps	
failures	success	

Can you complete these sentences using the words from the puzzle?

* Cel_____ your mistakes and f_____, as steps toward your next success.

* Never stop t_____, celebrate your wins as well as your tries. Tr____ again means you have learnt something new.

b	a	x	t	e	r	q	w	e	r
e	f	a	i	l	u	r	e	s	z
s	v	c	s	z	p	m	b	v	c
t	a	i	u	o	l	i	f	e	m
b	s	r	c	e	d	s	p	o	i
m	t	n	c	b	v	t	g	t	r
c	e	l	e	b	r	a	t	e	z
z	p	v	s	m	n	k	v	a	c
f	s	t	s	r	e	e	g	c	z
t	r	y	i	n	g	s	q	h	m

"The more you celebrate your life,
the more there is in life to celebrate."
Oprah Winfrey

Lead by example.

In our story 'Baxter Learns to Fly'...

After being told that bumblebees can't fly by someone he admired, Baxter felt sad. When he got home, Mother Bumblebee listened patiently to Baxter. Then, she showed him that even though he did have small delicate wings, he could fly! She explained that bumblebees move their wings differently than other bugs so they can fly AND carry large amounts of pollen too!

Wisdom tip for parents and teachers:

As adults, we have invariably experienced the pain of negative words spoken to us by others. Perhaps these words have also limited or defined our current circumstances, but they don't have to. You can learn to fly too! Fly above the negative words of others and be all you were meant to be. We need to teach our children to believe they can fly, and one of the best ways to teach them this is to demonstrate that we too can fly above negative words and circumstances, so they can too.

"Tell me and I may forget, teach me and I may remember, involve me and I learn." Benjamin Franklin

Connection Point:

- Was there a time in your life that someone's negative words stopped you from trying or doing something? Why not give it a go now? Tell your child what the negative words were and involve them in your venture of trying anyway or trying again.

- Talk to your child about any negative words that have been spoken to them. Embark on an adventure together to show them that these words don't define them. They are unique so they should celebrate that and other people's negative words do not define them!

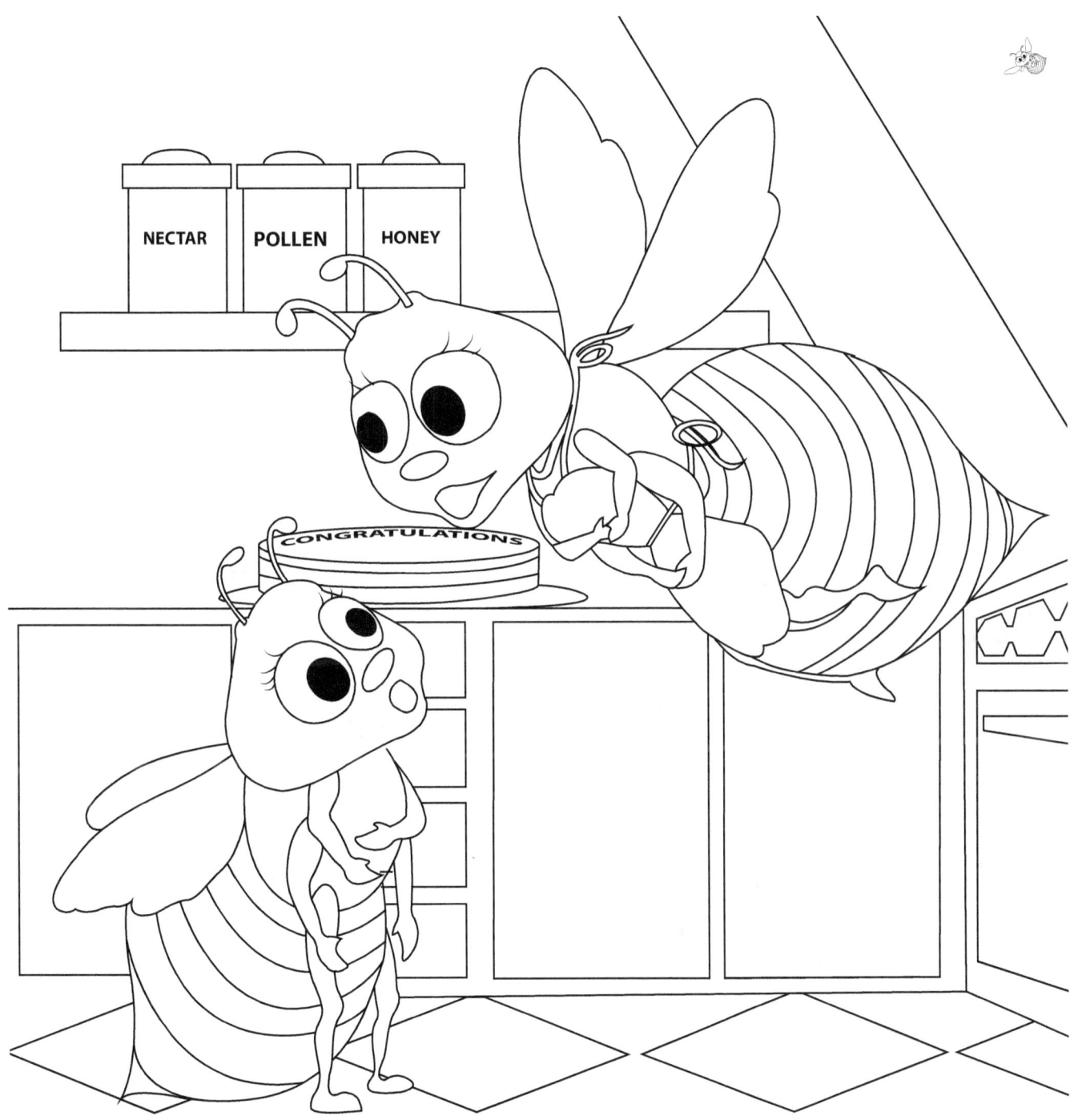

Lead by example!

Can you find these words in the puzzle?

baxter	lead	think
believe	limit	words
example	negative	
experience	show	

Can you complete these sentences using the words from the puzzle?

* Be_____ in yourself, th___ positively and always lead by your exa____.

* B_____'s mum lead by exa____ and showed him bumblebees could fly!

62

e	x	p	e	r	i	e	n	c	e
z	w	v	b	a	x	t	e	r	s
q	o	l	e	a	d	w	e	r	h
v	r	r	l	i	m	i	t	z	o
n	d	c	i	b	m	s	h	o	w
n	s	n	e	g	a	t	i	v	e
w	e	r	v	t	h	i	n	k	m
m	n	b	e	x	a	m	p	l	e

"The world is changed by your example, not by your opinion."
Paulo Coelho

Courage to try again!

In our story 'Baxter Learns to Fly'...

Mother Bumblebee showed Baxter that bumblebees really can fly, and after this, Baxter decided he was going to go back to 'Bug Flying School' to learn to fly with Lydia and Boston. After listening to Maxwell, Baxter felt sad, but now he had new hope in his heart because his mother showed him it was possible for bumblebees to fly even with their tiny, delicate wings! With renewed hope, Baxter was determined to try again.

Wisdom tip for parents and teachers:

Building resilience, persistence and the confidence to try again are important lessons for us all to learn. When we encounter difficulties in life (rest assured, we all will), we must develop the ability to get up, dust ourselves off and try again. We must develop the confidence to persist until we see results or are comfortable with our efforts. Life doesn't always go as planned, but if we give up too easily or too soon, who knows the joys, successes and rewards we may miss out on. As parents and teachers, it is important that we set the example in our own lives too. Don't ever fear failure; it is the stepping stone that brings you closer to success!

Connection Point:

- Using Baxter as an example, take this opportunity to talk to your children about trying again.
- Write a list of things they are finding challenging and make a plan to try again...and again, if needed! Don't give up! Be deliberate about celebrating their attempts too, not just the wins.

Courage to try again!

Can you find these words in the puzzle?

again	courage	lydia
baxter	determined	try
boston	fearless	
brave	help	

Can you complete these sentences using the words from the puzzle?

* I am fea_____! If I make a mistake or fail, I will get up, dust myself off and t__ again!

* L___a and Bo____ were determ____ to encourage Baxter to try again.

q	f	a	g	a	i	n	w	e	t
d	e	t	e	r	m	i	n	e	d
b	a	x	t	e	r	z	x	c	l
v	r	b	o	s	t	o	n	b	y
d	l	h	e	l	p	m	n	r	d
f	e	a	r	l	e	s	s	a	i
v	s	c	t	r	y	v	c	v	a
z	s	c	o	u	r	a	g	e	z

"Your dream doesn't have an expiration date.
Take a big breath and try again!"
K T Witten

Celebrate what you are good at!

In our story 'Baxter Learns to Fly'...

When Baxter and his friends were walking to 'Bug Flying School' they came across some friends. One friend, Susie the Spider, was happily spinning her web in the sun. Baxter told Susie that he, Boston and Lydia were going to learn to fly. Susie was happy for the three bugs and encouraged them.

Wisdom tip for parents and teachers:

Sometimes, it's easy to wish we were the same as those around us, but quite simply, we are not. We are all different and we all have different skills and talents. Susie the Spider could have said, "I wish I could fly. Why can't I fly? Why do I have to spend my days spinning web after web?", but she didn't. She was happy for Baxter, Boston and Lydia to go and learn to fly, and she was happy to keep spinning her webs.

It is important to learn that we won't be good at everything, so we shouldn't compare ourselves to others. It is important to try new things, but we should <u>celebrate what we are good at.</u>

Connection Point:

- Make a list with your child. Write down what each of you enjoy doing and what you are good at. The next time you do something you are good at, be sure to celebrate.

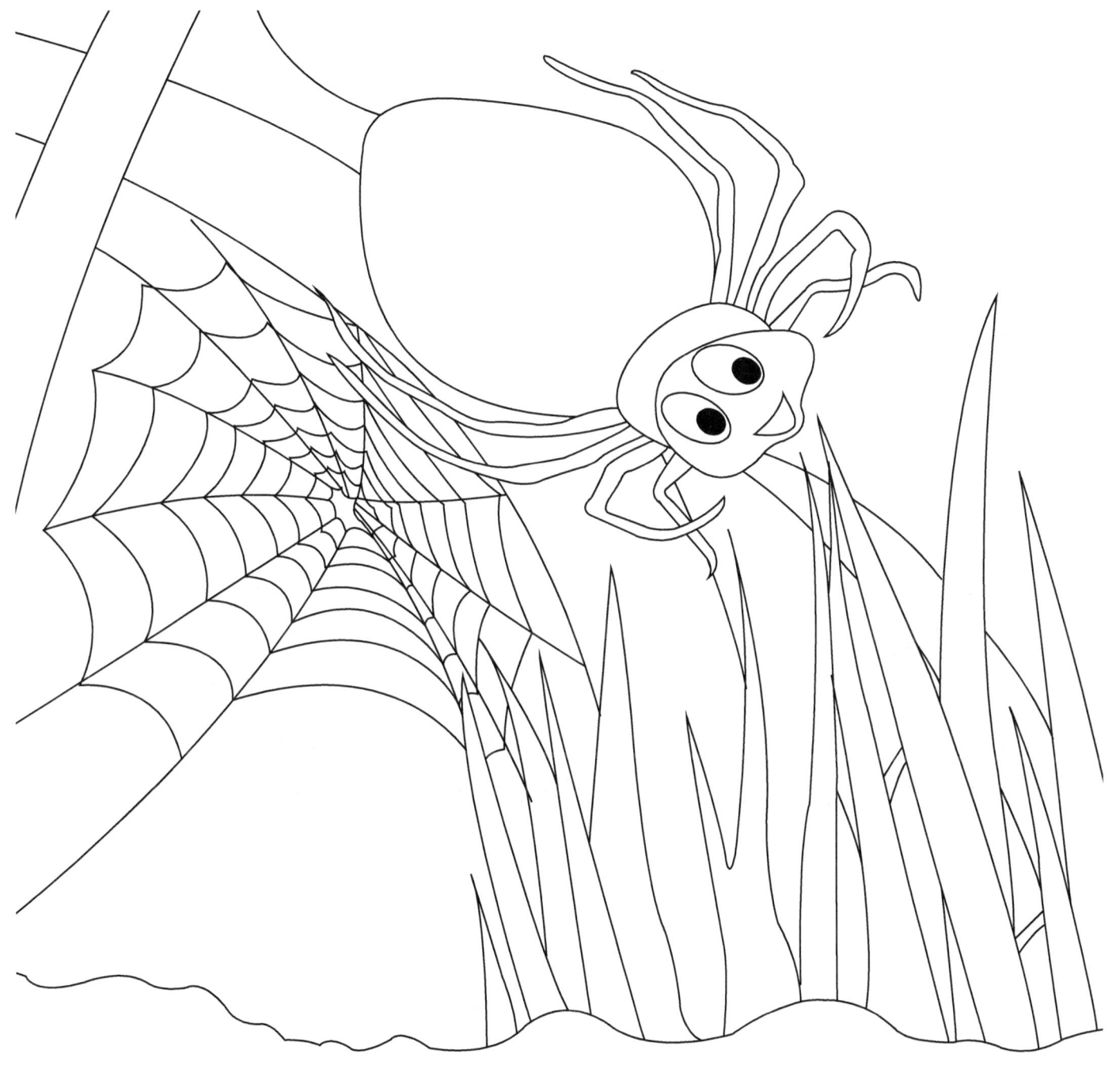

Celebrate what you are good at!

Can you find these words in the puzzle?

baxter	fly	unique
boston	good	webs
celebrate	spider	
different	susie	

Can you complete these sentences using the words from the puzzle?

* We are all dif____nt. Find what you are g___ at and cel____te it. Being different is awesome!

* Sus__ the Spi___ was different to Bax___. Susie spun w___ and Baxter could f__.

d	i	f	f	e	r	e	n	t	a
z	c	e	l	e	b	r	a	t	e
s	x	c	y	b	a	x	t	e	r
u	f	g	o	o	d	v	b	w	t
s	q	w	e	s	p	i	d	e	r
i	z	x	c	t	f	g	h	b	o
e	p	a	q	o	c	v	r	s	e
f	d	f	u	n	i	q	u	e	m

"You have to be unique and different, and shine in your own way!"
Lady Gaga

Be Patient.

In our story 'Baxter Learns to Fly'...

Baxter met Casper the Caterpillar on his way to 'Bug Flying School'. Casper was busy eating his breakfast of green grass and leaves so he didn't have time to stop and talk to Baxter, Lydia and Boston. Baxter told Casper that he, Lydia and Boston were going to learn to fly, and Casper was happy for them.

Wisdom tip for parents and teachers:

Casper was a caterpillar, and one day, he would turn into a butterfly. But for now, he had to wait and be content with being a caterpillar. Casper wanted to fly, and inside, he knew he was meant to fly...just not yet.

Sometimes, we have to wait a little longer or try a little harder than others before we get what we want or can do what they can do. That is okay. Life is not the same for everybody. We are all different. We all learn and develop at different rates. Your turn to shine will come!

Connection Point:

- Talk to your child about qualities or abilities where they are struggling or having to try harder than some others.

- Talk about those skills or abilities that may improve over time. Having to wait is an opportunity to learn patience.

- Using Casper as an example, discuss with your child that being patient gives us an opportunity to let others help us as well as the opportunity to practise and try again!

Be patient.

Can you find these words in the puzzle?

baxter	goals	wait
boston	hard	work
casper	patiently	
caterpillar	quietly	

Can you complete these sentences using the words from the puzzle?

* Sometimes we must w___ pat____ly.

* Cas___ the Ca___pillar had to wait patiently to learn to fly. One day he will w___ hard to spin a cocoon. When he comes out of the cocoon he can learn to fly with his new wings.

b	o	s	t	o	n	z	v	b	b	a
c	a	t	e	r	p	i	l	l	a	r
q	u	i	e	t	l	y	a	s	x	p
q	w	e	r	t	y	w	a	i	t	o
k	h	j	h	g	c	a	s	p	e	r
p	a	t	i	e	n	t	l	y	r	z
v	r	b	n	m	g	g	o	a	l	s
g	d	d	s	w	o	r	k	s	e	w

"Slow and Steady wins the race.
Be patient, work hard and never lose sight of your goals."
Author unknown

Asking for help and taking advice

In our story 'Baxter Learns to Fly'...

When Baxter, Lydia and Boston arrived at 'Bug Flying School', Grasshopper Teacher taught them about bugs that can fly. Some bugs fly by moving their wings up and down, and some, like butterflies, move theirs in a figure 8 pattern. Baxter, Lydia and Boston enjoyed learning about how different bugs move their wings to fly. Wise Grasshopper Teacher was a trusted advisor that Baxter, Lydia and Boston could learn from as well as turn to for help and advice.

Wisdom tip for parents and teachers:

It is important that children learn to seek and take advice from parents, teachers and other trusted friends. Asking for help is good. It can improve our skills, knowledge and confidence... and this goes for the big kids as well! However, children can be very trusting, so it is up to us as their carers to ensure that they know who to go to to learn something new, who can answer their questions, and where to go if they need help or advice. Baxter, Lydia and Boston trusted Grasshopper Teacher so they felt comfortable asking him questions to learn more.

Connection Point:

- Using Baxter, Lydia and Boston as examples, spend some time talking to your children about what a trusted person is, and who is a trusted person in their lives from whom they can seek help.

- Now, spend some time talking to your children about safe places to go if they need help or advice or if they have questions to ask.

- Make a 'contacts' list with your children of people they can trust, safe places to go to and phone numbers to call.

Asking for help and taking advice

Can you find these words in the puzzle?

advice	confidence	knowledge
ask	grasshopper	skills
baxter	help	
boston	instruction	

Can you complete these sentences using the words from the puzzle?

* Asking for h___ and taking ad____ will improve my know_____ and confidence.

* Grass_____ Teacher taught Ba____, Bo____ and Lydia how all bugs fly so they could h___ each other.

q	w	e	r	t	y	c	h	e	l	p
g	r	a	s	s	h	o	p	p	e	r
c	v	s	z	x	c	n	v	b	s	s
f	d	k	g	h	j	f	e	r	t	y
f	g	h	d	s	k	i	l	l	s	t
k	n	o	w	l	e	d	g	e	h	g
m	a	d	v	i	c	e	r	t	y	u
v	b	o	s	t	o	n	b	v	z	z
i	n	s	t	r	u	c	t	i	o	n
d	f	b	a	x	t	e	r	t	r	e

"The mind that opens to a new idea never returns to its original size."
Albert Einstein

Learn about others - understand differences

In our story 'Baxter Learns to Fly'...

When Baxter, Lydia and Boston were at 'Bug Flying School', they learned how each of them moved their wings to fly. Lydia moved her wings forward and backward. Boston moved his large, wide wings in a figure 8 pattern. Baxter moved his wings like a helicopter—around and around above him. This helps bumblebees hover in one place and then move backwards, forwards and sideways.

Wisdom tip for parents and teachers:

Baxter learned how his friends moved their wings to fly. It is important for children to learn about others, understand their differences and always respect each other. Differences may be in physical appearance, ability, cultural background, language or something else. When you learn about differences, it removes fear of the unknown and helps us to embrace new and exciting things about one another and our surroundings. It also helps us build knowledge as well as social and emotional intelligence. If we take our children through this process, it shows them that embracing differences is good and exciting, and it also allows us to teach them safely.

Connection Point:

- Using Baxter as an example, ask your children about someone they know who is different from them in some way. They may be different in their looks, abilities, culture, the way they dress or their language.

- Spend some time with your children learning about these differences and then help them frame a genuine compliment such as: "I like your red hair" or, "You are very clever to speak another language."

Learn about others - understand differences

Can you find these words in the puzzle?

baxter   learn   understand
boston   others   unique
differences   recognise
enjoy   respect

Can you complete these sentences using the words from the puzzle?

* It is important to l____ about our diff_____. This helps us to under_____, respect and en___ each other more.

* The three bugs learned they were each un____ in their own way.

r	e	s	p	e	c	t	b	z	x	c
u	n	d	e	r	s	t	a	n	d	z
z	x	c	n	q	w	e	x	g	h	j
b	n	b	j	z	x	c	t	p	o	a
a	s	d	o	h	j	k	e	m	t	b
n	b	v	y	l	e	a	r	n	h	o
d	i	f	f	e	r	e	n	c	e	s
u	n	i	q	u	e	f	d	s	r	t
b	v	c	x	o	t	h	e	r	s	o
r	e	c	o	g	n	i	s	e	g	n

"The ability to recognise and respect individual differences is the beginning of a successful relationship."
Aniekee Tochukwu

Hope and Confidence

In our story 'Baxter Learns to Fly'...

When Baxter joined Boston and Lydia at 'Bug Flying School', he learned exactly how bumblebees fly. Bumblebees beat their wings up to 200 times per second and move them like a helicopter. Bumblebees actually hover and can move forwards, backwards and sideways. They have strong muscles in their chests where their wings are connected; all this allows them to fly and carry large amounts of pollen to make honey.

It was important for Baxter to learn exactly how he flies, not just for the practicalities of flying, but it raised his hopes and built his confidence.

Wisdom tip for parents and teachers:

Hope and confidence are the springboards to achieve your dreams. Irrespective of your abilities or disabilities, we can all dream and we can all achieve something great. It is fear and disappointment that limit us. American President Theodore Roosevelt (who needed a wheelchair) said, "Believe you can, and you are halfway there." Baxter had to learn how bumblebees flew, and this helped him believe he could fly!

Connection Point:

- Using Baxter as an example, speak honestly with your children about their dreams or things they want to accomplish. It may be to complete a maths problem, climb a tree, recite a poem or move independently from one room to another.

- Help your child learn what is involved with accomplishing their goal, and then help them by making a plan to improve their skills. Build their hope and confidence through encouragement, and then practise, practise, practise.

Hope and Confidence

Can you find these words in the puzzle?

achieve	faith	trust
baxter	hope	try
boston	lydia	
confidence	optimistic	

Can you complete these sentences using the words from the puzzle?

* H___ and con_____ will help me achieve my goals. I can do it!

* Lydia and Boston had f____ Baxter could learn to fly, and they were right!

a	c	o	n	f	i	d	e	n	c	e
q	w	p	r	t	y	u	i	o	p	z
c	v	t	r	u	s	t	n	m	h	g
f	a	i	t	h	b	a	x	t	e	r
s	s	m	z	c	v	h	g	t	r	e
t	y	i	r	f	b	o	s	t	o	n
v	f	s	r	e	x	p	a	t	r	e
b	n	t	r	y	t	e	r	e	w	z
b	v	i	c	x	h	l	y	d	i	a
g	a	c	h	i	e	v	e	v	c	x

"Optimism is the faith that leads to achievement. Nothing can be done without hope and confidence."
Helen Keller

Learning new things and asking lots of questions

In our story 'Baxter Learns to Fly'...

Baxter, Lydia and Boston all went to 'Bug Flying School' together. It was important for them to learn how each of the bugs moved their wings to fly so they could help and encourage each other when practising. The three bugs were best friends so learning together and asking lots of questions was important and much more fun!

Wisdom tip for parents and teachers:

Learning together with friends and engaging in group dialogue can support and enhance learning. It not only opens our minds up to diversity and appreciating differences, but it can support inquiry and critical thinking. Sharing and refining ideas with friends also supports and reinforces the development of new skills. Baxter, Lydia and Boston all used their wings differently to fly and now, they could all encourage each other to move their wings the way they were meant to.

Connection Point:

- Using Baxter, Boston and Lydia as examples, spend some time with your children talking about the benefits of learning in groups or with friends, and not being afraid to ask questions or say, "I don't understand, please help me."

- Encourage your children to learn about others, learn new ways of doing things and never be afraid to ask lots of questions to learn more.

Learning new things and asking lots of questions

Can you find these words in the puzzle?

asking	learn	questions
baxter	lydia	quiz
boston	study	
inquire	query	

Can you complete these sentences using the words from the puzzle?

* As____ a lot of que_____ helps me l____ more.

* Ba____, Bo____ and Ly___ went to 'Bug Flying School'. They asked lots of qu_____ to help them l____ more about flying.

a	i	q	u	i	z	d	f	g	b	z
m	n	s	b	a	x	t	e	r	o	n
t	q	u	e	s	t	i	o	n	s	r
b	u	s	n	k	t	q	r	e	t	d
v	i	t	t	i	z	u	n	b	o	v
t	r	u	r	n	l	e	a	r	n	s
v	e	d	r	g	z	r	q	u	b	n
l	l	y	d	i	a	y	s	s	t	h

"The beautiful thing about learning is nobody can take it away from you!"
B B King

A Wise Proverb

"The tongue has the power of life and death.
The stakes are high.
Your words can either speak life,
or your words can speak death.
Our tongues can build others up,
or they can tear them down."

Did you find all 26 tiny pictures of Baxter?

www.ingramcontent.com/pod-product-compliance
Lightning Source LLC
Chambersburg PA
CBHW060533010526
44107CB00059B/2631